Use the QR code to follow along on YouTube or visit @Politheoctopus on YouTube to hear the book read to you!

Dedicated to the ones who created and shaped me, Jerry and Joycelyn Weems. To those that inadvertently raised me, the VIP crew- Imani, Miriah, D.Xavier-Jevon, Maurice. And to those who inspired me, Prince and Mr.FINE. I hope to always give my best to you.

Poli The Octopus
Your Multilingual pal
Children's Book Series

Head of Illustrations Imani Weems Earskines

Hello!

¡Hola!

My name is Poli

Me llamo Poli

I am an Octopus

Soy un pulpo

I live in the water

Vivo en el agua

I have eight
arms

Tengo ocho brazos

I eat crabs and lobsters

Como cangrejos
y langostas

I like to
swim

Me gusta nadar

I can change colors

Puedo cambiar de color

Nice to
meet you

Encantado
de conocerte

Goodbye!

¡Adiós!

www.ingramcontent.com/pod-product-compliance
Lightning Source LLC
LaVergne TN
LVHW072133070426

835513LV00002B/95